THE HUMAN BODY
QUESTIONS & ANSWERS

ANGELA ROYSTON

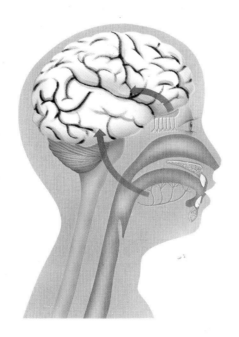

Kingfisher

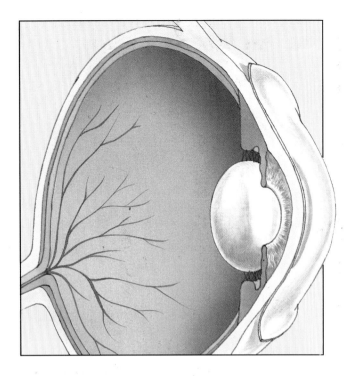

CONTENTS

KINGFISHER
An imprint of Larousse plc
Elsley House, 24–30 Great Titchfield Street,
London W1P 7AD

This edition published by Kingfisher 1995

10 9 8 7 6 5 4 3 2 1

Copyright © Larousse plc 1995

Originally published by Kingfisher 1990 in the
Tell Me About series
Copyright © Grisewood & Dempsey Ltd 1990

A CIP catalogue record for this book is available from the
British Library

ISBN 1 85697 368 9

Series editor: Jackie Gaff
Series designer: Terry Woodley
Author: Angela Royston
Consultant: Brian Ward
Designer: David West Children's Book Design
Illustrators: Chris Forsey (pp. 9, 15, 22–3, 28–30, 33 top,
38); Rob Shone (pp. 2–8, 10–14, 16–21, 24–7, 31–7)
Cover illustration: Chris Forsey
Phototypeset by Southern Positives and Negatives
(SPAN), Lingfield, Surrey
Printed and bound in Spain

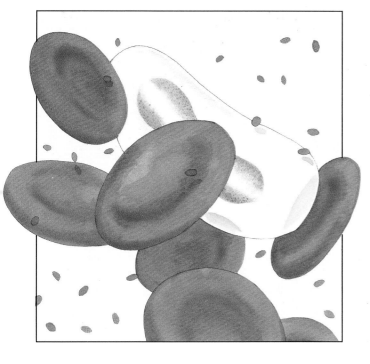

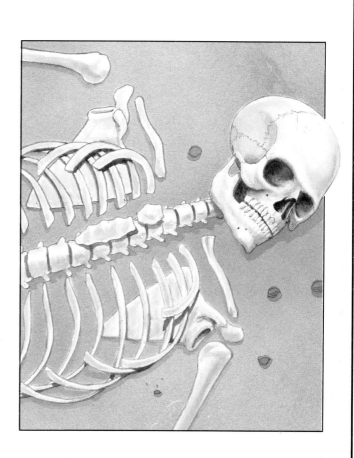

Our bodies are made of millions of tiny living units called cells, most of them too small to be seen without a microscope. These cells are the building blocks from which everything else is made – bones, blood, muscles, skin, and all the other parts of the body. There are lots of different sorts of cell, and each type has its own special job to do.

DO YOU KNOW

Around 18% of your body is made of carbon, which is the same material that diamonds and pencil leads are made of! As well, your body contains calcium (also found in chalk) and phosphorus, which is used in making safety matches. There is even some iron!

BODY FACTS

● Your body is mainly made of water – water accounts for 70% of your weight, in fact.

● Your heart is a muscle which pumps blood around your body. An adult's heart beats over 100,000 times each day.

● Cells come in all shapes and sizes – some are round, some are flat, some are square. Most cells have a control centre called a nucleus, which keeps the cell alive and doing its own special job. New cells are made when one cell divides.

Nucleus

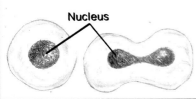

Bones support your body's weight and give it shape. Without bones you would collapse in a heap.

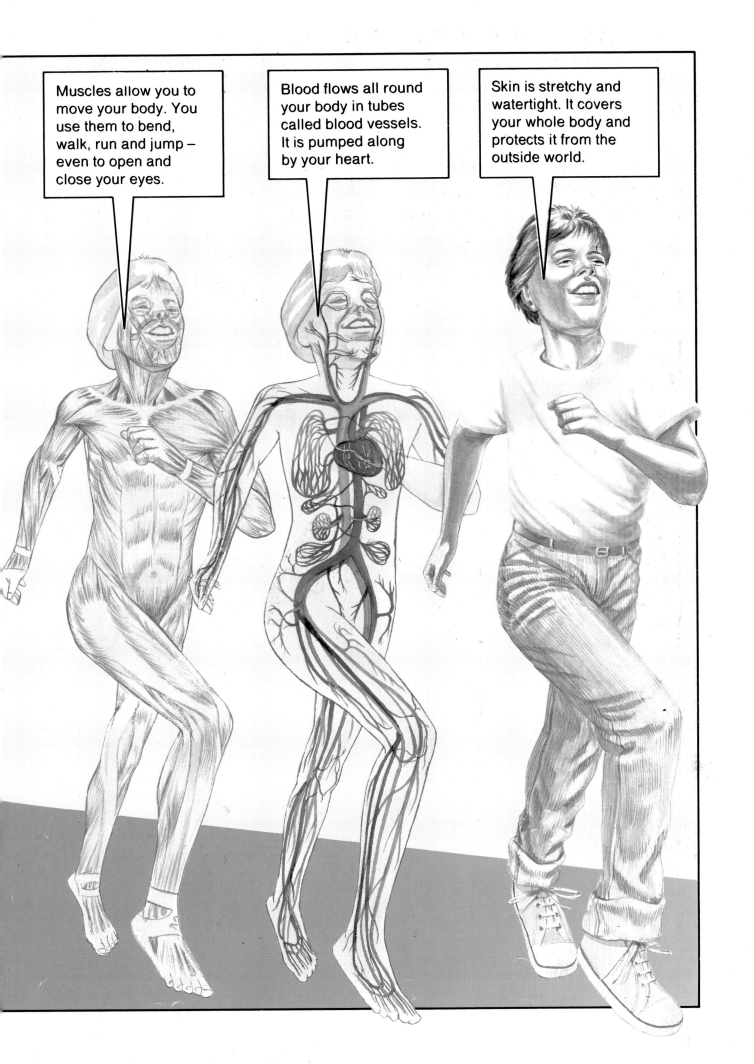

HOW MANY BONES DO WE HAVE?

By the time we are fully grown we have about 206 different bones, but when we were born we had around 350. This is because many smaller bones join together as we grow.

Bones make a framework called the skeleton, which supports the body and carries its weight. Some bones also protect important parts of the body from being injured – the skull protects the brain, for example.

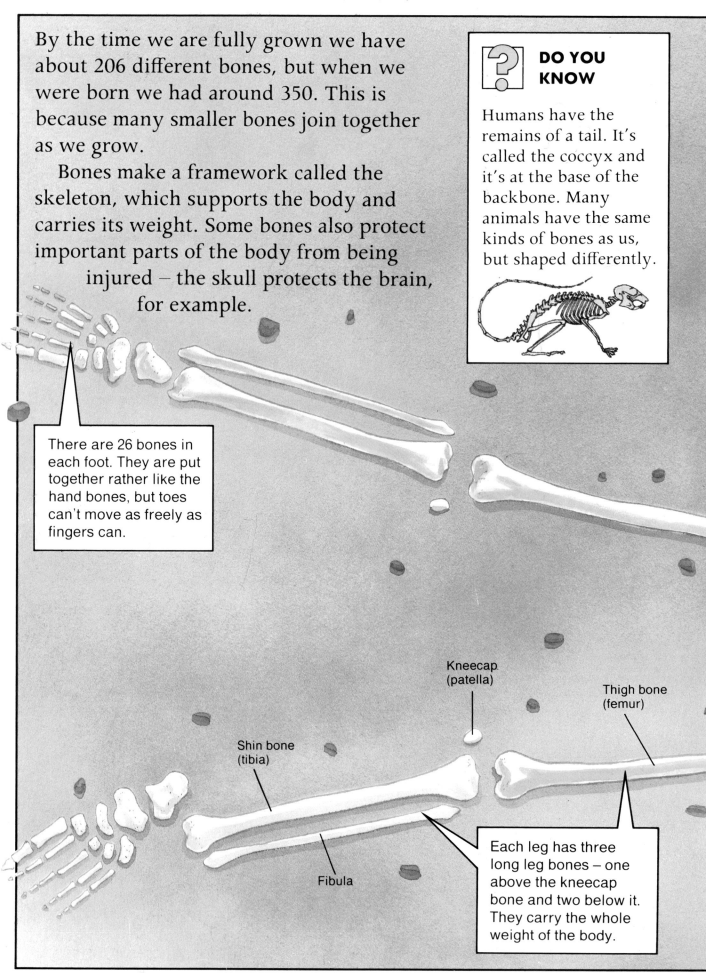

DO YOU KNOW

Humans have the remains of a tail. It's called the coccyx and it's at the base of the backbone. Many animals have the same kinds of bones as us, but shaped differently.

There are 26 bones in each foot. They are put together rather like the hand bones, but toes can't move as freely as fingers can.

Kneecap (patella)

Thigh bone (femur)

Shin bone (tibia)

Fibula

Each leg has three long leg bones – one above the kneecap bone and two below it. They carry the whole weight of the body.

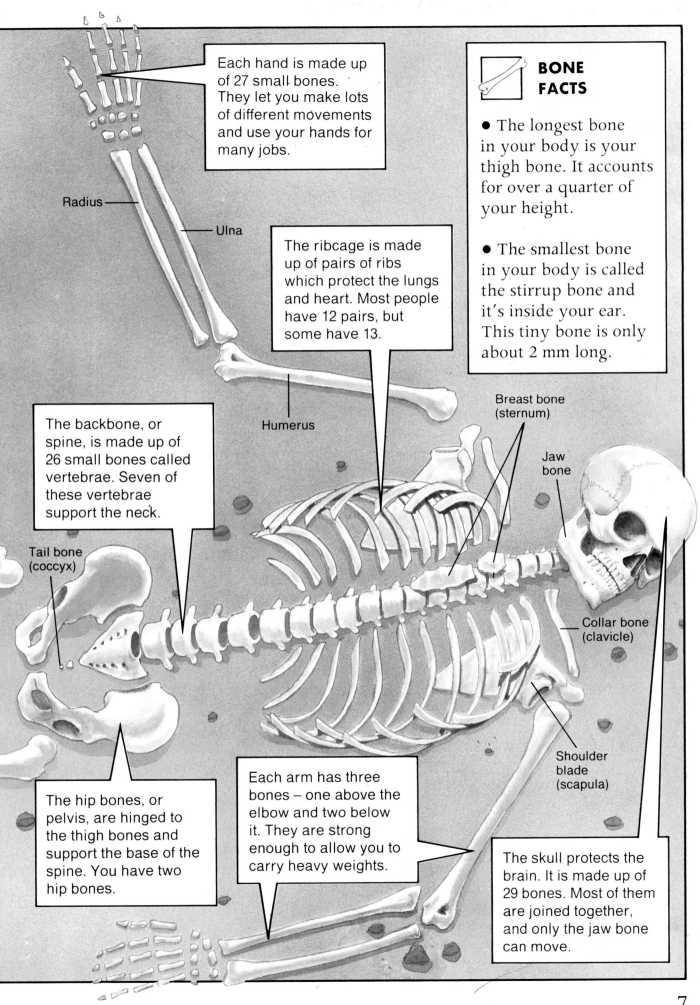

Each hand is made up of 27 small bones. They let you make lots of different movements and use your hands for many jobs.

Radius

Ulna

The ribcage is made up of pairs of ribs which protect the lungs and heart. Most people have 12 pairs, but some have 13.

Humerus

The backbone, or spine, is made up of 26 small bones called vertebrae. Seven of these vertebrae support the neck.

Tail bone (coccyx)

The hip bones, or pelvis, are hinged to the thigh bones and support the base of the spine. You have two hip bones.

Each arm has three bones – one above the elbow and two below it. They are strong enough to allow you to carry heavy weights.

BONE FACTS

● The longest bone in your body is your thigh bone. It accounts for over a quarter of your height.

● The smallest bone in your body is called the stirrup bone and it's inside your ear. This tiny bone is only about 2 mm long.

Breast bone (sternum)

Jaw bone

Collar bone (clavicle)

Shoulder blade (scapula)

The skull protects the brain. It is made up of 29 bones. Most of them are joined together, and only the jaw bone can move.

WHAT ARE BONES LIKE INSIDE?

Our bones are hard and strong because they are partly made of a stony material. Unlike stones, though, bones are neither solid nor dead. They are more like strong tubes which carry blood and other living material inside them. Bones are made by living cells, and they can grow and mend themselves if they get cracked or broken.

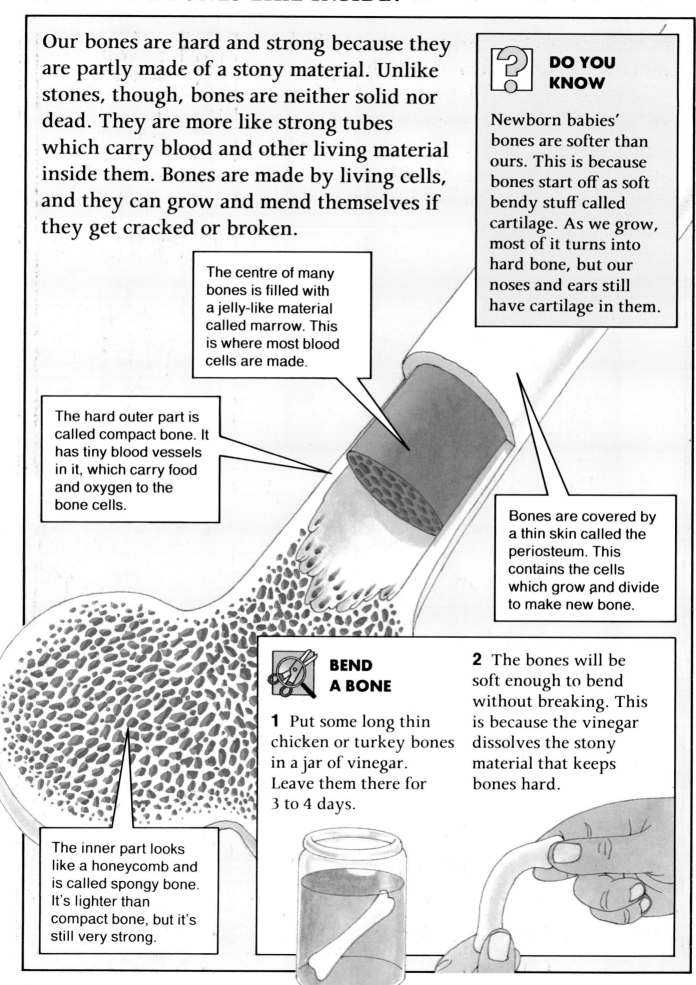

? DO YOU KNOW

Newborn babies' bones are softer than ours. This is because bones start off as soft bendy stuff called cartilage. As we grow, most of it turns into hard bone, but our noses and ears still have cartilage in them.

The centre of many bones is filled with a jelly-like material called marrow. This is where most blood cells are made.

The hard outer part is called compact bone. It has tiny blood vessels in it, which carry food and oxygen to the bone cells.

Bones are covered by a thin skin called the periosteum. This contains the cells which grow and divide to make new bone.

The inner part looks like a honeycomb and is called spongy bone. It's lighter than compact bone, but it's still very strong.

BEND A BONE

1 Put some long thin chicken or turkey bones in a jar of vinegar. Leave them there for 3 to 4 days.

2 The bones will be soft enough to bend without breaking. This is because the vinegar dissolves the stony material that keeps bones hard.

HOW DO JOINTS WORK?

The place where two bones meet is called a joint. Some bones are fixed firmly together – the ones in the skull, for example – but our bodies also have several kinds of movable joint. These allow us to bend, twist and turn various parts of our bodies. Two of the main kinds of movable joint are illustrated below.

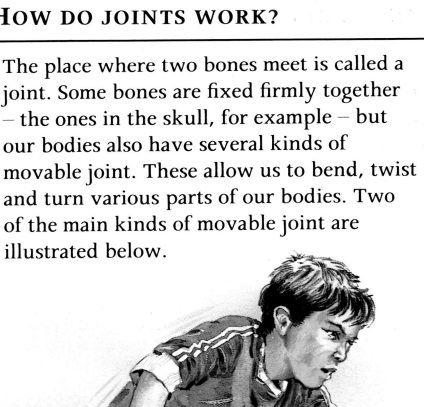

DO YOU KNOW

Many joints are 'oiled' with a liquid called synovial fluid to help them move. The bone heads are cushioned with cartilage and held in place by straps called ligaments.

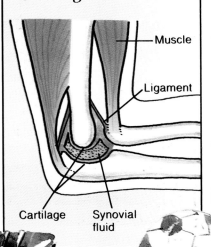

Muscle

Ligament

Cartilage   Synovial fluid

Did you know that you are about 1 cm shorter in the evening than when you wake in the morning? Each of the 26 bones in your spine is separated by a disc, or pad, of cartilage. As you walk about during the day, the weight of your upper body squashes the discs – this is what makes you a little shorter by the time evening comes.

HINGE JOINT

Your elbows and knees have hinge joints. Joints like these bend and straighten just like a door swinging on its hinges.

BALL-AND-SOCKET JOINT

In a ball-and-socket joint, the round end of one bone fits into a hollow in another bone. Shoulders and hips have ball-and-socket joints.

All the movements our bodies make depend on muscles – even when we are standing still, we are using muscles in our backs, necks, arms and legs to stay upright. Many of our muscles work without our thinking about them, like the ones we use in breathing and in digesting our food.

Most things we do take many muscles working together. This is because muscles can't push, they can only pull. You can see how muscles work together in the diagram opposite.

MUSCLE FACTS

● Your body has more than 650 muscles.

● You use 200 muscles every time you take a step.

● There are more than 30 muscles in your face. It takes 15 muscles to smile.

The weight-lifter bends his knees and positions his feet apart, so that he can use his leg and back muscles as well as his arms to help lift and carry the weight of the dumbbell.

Weight-lifters need very powerful muscles. Exercise makes muscles bigger and stronger.

Because muscles can only pull, not push, they often work in pairs. One muscle shortens to pull a bone one way, then another muscle pulls the bone back again.

Biceps muscle

Radius bone

1

Muscles are attached to bones by tendons

1 To bend the arm, the biceps shortens and pulls up the radius bone.

2 To straighten the arm, the biceps relaxes and the triceps shortens.

2

Biceps muscle

Triceps muscle

Doctors use Latin names to identify different muscles.

Deltoid (shoulder)

Latissimus dorsi (rib)

Rectus femoris (thigh)

Gastrocnemius (calf)

Sternomastoid (neck)

Pectoralis major (breast)

Rectus abdominus (stomach)

Peroneus brevis (ankle)

? DO YOU KNOW

We all have muscles for waggling our ears! There is one behind each ear, but most of us never learn to use them. We can't waggle our ears because muscles that don't get exercised become weak and can't be used.

HOW FAST CAN PEOPLE RUN?

The fastest race is the 100-metre sprint, and the best male runners can finish it in less than 10 seconds – that's 36 km/h. The fastest women runners take just over half a second longer.

RUNNING FACTS

● In 1954 Roger Bannister of Great Britain became the first person to run a mile (1609 m) in less than 4 minutes. Bannister's actual time was 3 minutes 59.4 seconds.

● The longest race is the marathon, with a distance of 42.2 km. The fastest marathon runners average nearly 20 km/h.

HOW HIGH CAN PEOPLE JUMP?

The best high-jumpers can jump more than their own height – well over 2 metres. They use the Fosbury flop, the technique shown below, which was invented by Dick Fosbury in 1968. Using a pole helps the best pole-vaulters to clear about 6 metres.

To cushion their fall, high-jumpers land on deep padded mats or air-filled mattresses.

For the Fosbury flop, the high-jumper turns his back to the bar. He arches his back over the bar as he jumps, and kicks his legs out to clear it. He lands on the mat on his shoulders and his back.

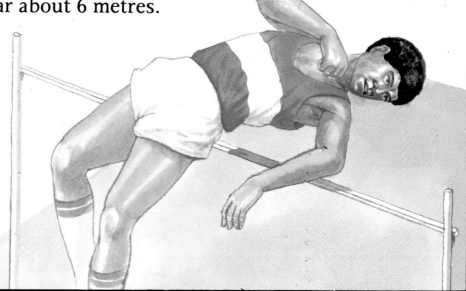

HOW FAR CAN PEOPLE JUMP?

From 1968 to 1991 the men's world long jump record was held by Bob Beamon, who jumped 8.9 metres during the Olympic Games in Mexico City. His record was broken by an 8.95-metre-jump by Mike Powell. The women's long jump record is just over 7.5 metres.

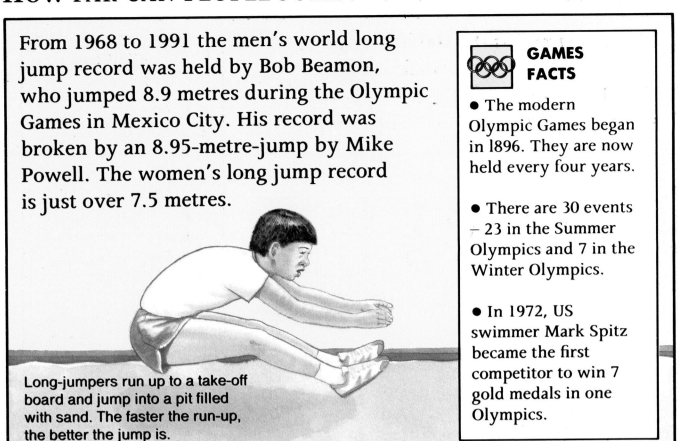

Long-jumpers run up to a take-off board and jump into a pit filled with sand. The faster the run-up, the better the jump is.

GAMES FACTS

● The modern Olympic Games began in 1896. They are now held every four years.

● There are 30 events – 23 in the Summer Olympics and 7 in the Winter Olympics.

● In 1972, US swimmer Mark Spitz became the first competitor to win 7 gold medals in one Olympics.

HOW FAST CAN PEOPLE SWIM?

The fastest male swimmers can cover 50 metres in a swimming pool in under 22 seconds – that's 8.2 km/h. The fastest women swimmers take about 3 seconds longer. To go this fast, swimmers use a stroke called freestyle.

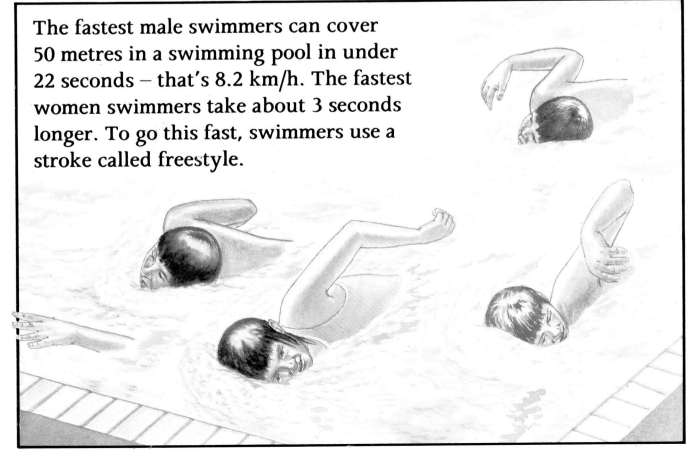

When we breathe air into our lungs, our bodies take a gas called oxygen from it. The oxygen passes from the lungs into the blood and is then carried around the body. Body cells need oxygen to make energy – if cells are starved of oxygen, they run out of energy and die. We all need the oxygen in air to stay alive.

BREATHING FACTS

● We take in about 20,000 breaths a day.

● An adult's lungs hold 5 litres of air.

1 When you breathe in, air is drawn through your nose or mouth and down your windpipe. The air is warmed on the way.

2 Your windpipe branches into two bronchial tubes – one for each lung. Inside the lungs, the tubes divide again and again, becoming smaller and smaller.

You have two lungs, one in each side of your chest. You can feel them fill with air as you breathe in.

Lungs

3 The tiniest tubes in your lungs end in bunches of air sacs called alveoli. Each air sac is surrounded by tiny blood vessels. The air sacs and blood vessels have such thin walls that oxygen can pass through them into the blood.

Alveoli

Blood vessels

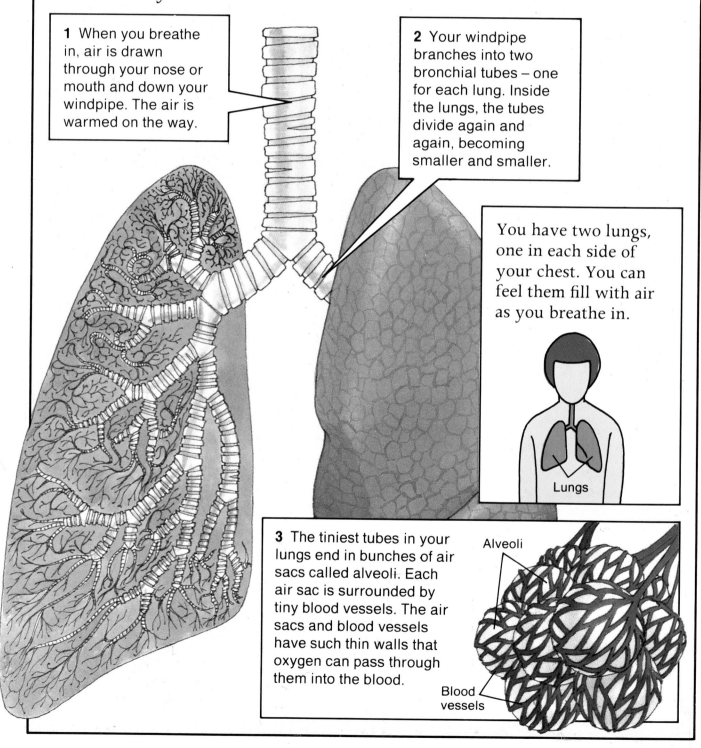

WHAT ARE HICCUPS?

Hiccups are short, sharp, and very sudden breaths of air. They happen when our breathing muscle jerks, making us gasp. Our lungs have no muscles of their own. Instead, they have a big muscle called the diaphragm below them. When the diaphragm pulls down, air is sucked into the lungs. When it relaxes, it forces air out.

DO YOU KNOW

When you sneeze, air rushes down your nose at over 160 km/h. You can't sneeze with your eyes open!

MEASURE YOUR BREATH

1 Ask an adult to help you fill an empty 2-litre bottle with water, 100 ml at a time. Mark each level on the side of the bottle.

2 Cover the top of the bottle and turn it upside down in a bowl which is half-full of water.

3 Put one end of a length of plastic tube into the neck of the bottle. Take a deep breath, then blow into the tube. How much water can your breath push out of the bottle?

As you breathe in (left), your diaphragm tightens and pulls down. Your rib muscles also tighten, making your ribs move up and out. This gives your lungs more space, which they fill by drawing in air.

AIR IN

Ribs

Diaphragm

AIR OUT

Your diaphragm relaxes and arches up to make you breathe out (right). Your rib muscles relax and your ribs move down and in. This forces some of the air out of your lungs.

WHY IS BLOOD RED?

Although blood looks red, it is largely made up of a yellowish liquid called plasma. Different sorts of blood cell float in the plasma – red cells, white cells, and tiny bits of cell called platelets. The red blood cells contain a substance called haemoglobin, which is the body's oxygen carrier. It is haemoglobin which gives red cells their colour and makes blood look red.

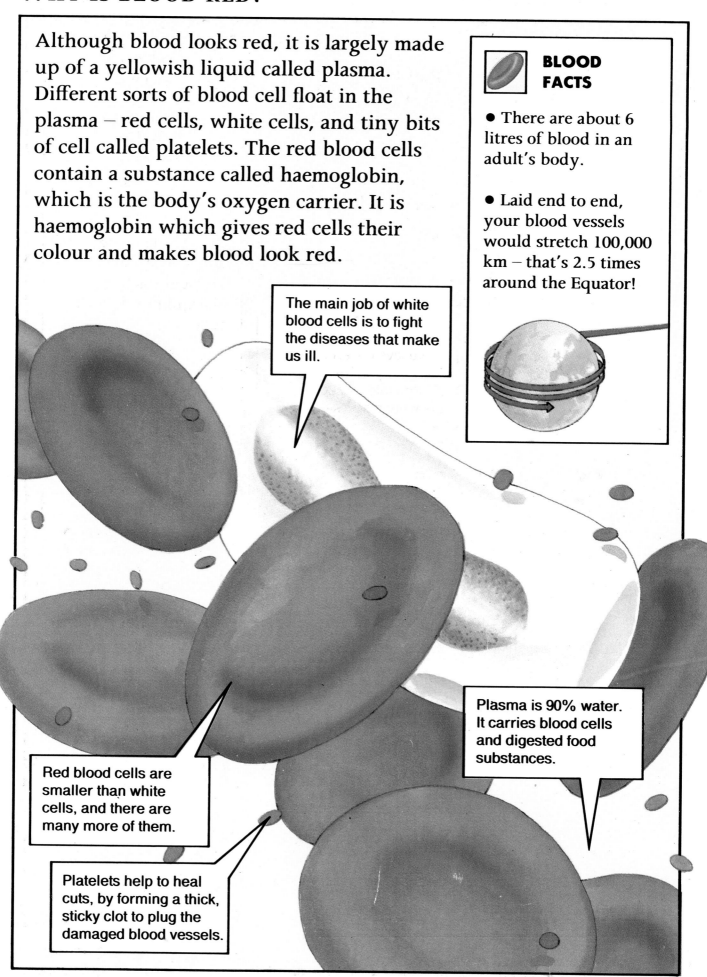

BLOOD FACTS

● There are about 6 litres of blood in an adult's body.

● Laid end to end, your blood vessels would stretch 100,000 km – that's 2.5 times around the Equator!

The main job of white blood cells is to fight the diseases that make us ill.

Plasma is 90% water. It carries blood cells and digested food substances.

Red blood cells are smaller than white cells, and there are many more of them.

Platelets help to heal cuts, by forming a thick, sticky clot to plug the damaged blood vessels.

HOW DO CUTS HEAL?

As soon as your skin is cut or grazed, your body starts to repair it. The platelets in your blood block breaks in the blood vessels just below the surface of the skin. They thicken and clot the blood, making it lumpy and plugging the breaks. The bleeding stops and the blood hardens into a scab. Fresh skin cells then grow through the wound, and after a while the scab falls off revealing shiny new shin.

DO YOU KNOW

Bruises form when blood vessels break and bleed under the skin – if you bump yourself, for example, but your skin isn't cut. As the blood clears away, the bruise turns from black to purple to yellow.

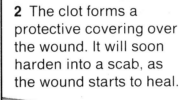

1 When you bleed, the blood helps to clean the wound. The bleeding will stop as platelets make the blood clot.

2 The clot forms a protective covering over the wound. It will soon harden into a scab, as the wound starts to heal.

3 New skin cells will grow under the scab. The new skin will look pink at first – you'll see it when the scab falls off.

DO YOU KNOW

People have different types of blood. There are four groups in all – A, B, AB and O. Blood groups are important when patients are given blood transfusions. People are usually given blood that matches their own blood type.

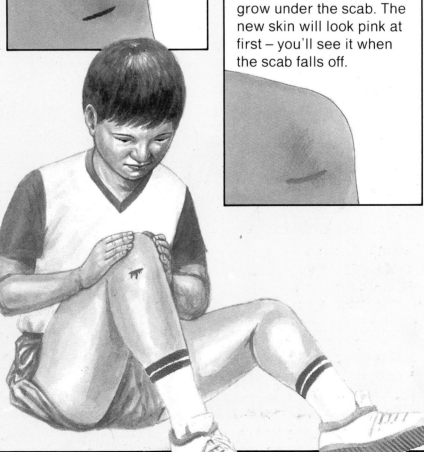

WHAT DOES THE HEART DO?

Your heart is a powerful muscle which pumps blood around your body, so that each cell gets the food and oxygen it needs. The left-hand side of the heart draws in oxygen-filled blood from the lungs and pumps it out again, round the body. The right-hand side takes in 'used' blood and sends it to the lungs to pick up a fresh supply of oxygen. Blood enters the heart in vessels called veins, and leaves it in arteries.

DO YOU KNOW

An adult human's heart usually beats about 70 times a minute. A mouse's heart beats about 500 times a minute, but an elephant's heart beats only about 25 times a minute!

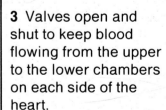

LISTEN TO HEART BEATS

1 Ask an adult to help you take the spout off an empty washing-up bottle and cut off the top of the bottle.

2 Push the end of a piece of plastic tubing over the neck of the bottle top.

3 Put the bottle top over a friend's heart, and hold the other end of the tube close to your ear. Can you hear a lub-dub lub-dub sound? It's made by the heart valves opening and shutting.

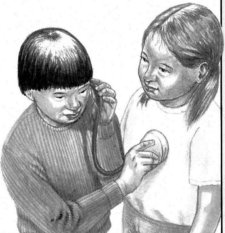

2 The blood flows from the vena cava into the upper right-hand chamber of the heart. This part is called the right atrium.

3 Valves open and shut to keep blood flowing from the upper to the lower chambers on each side of the heart.

DO YOU KNOW

Your heart is about the same size as your clenched fist. It's protected by your ribs and breastbone.

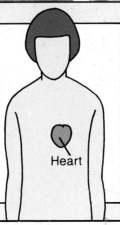

Heart

4 The lower right-hand chamber of the heart is called the right ventricle. From here, the 'used' blood is pumped to the lungs.

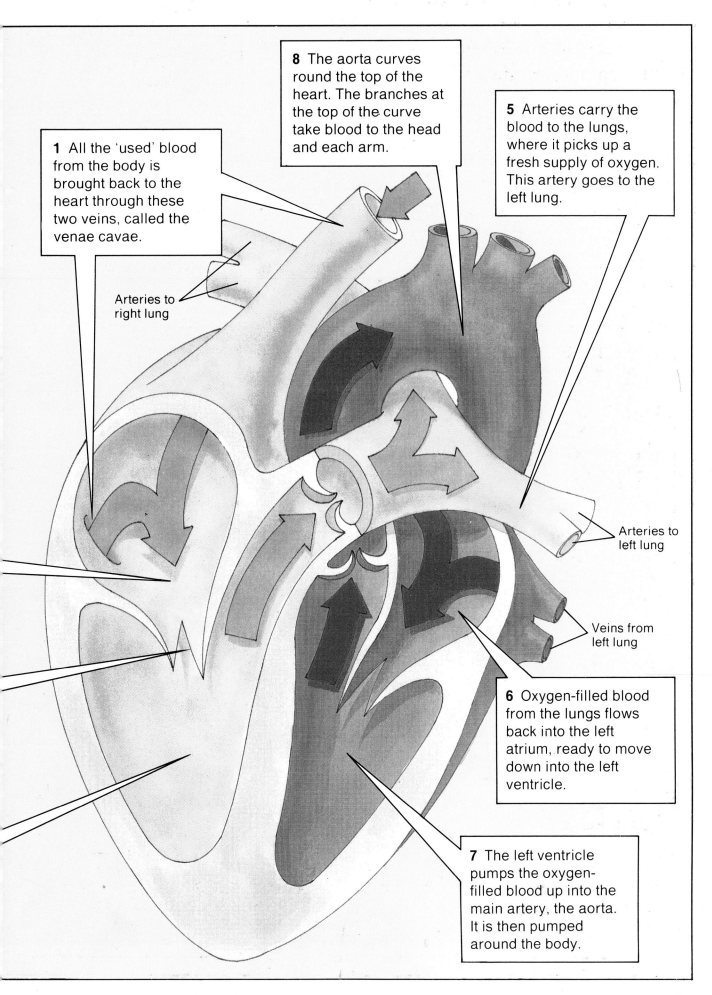

8 The aorta curves round the top of the heart. The branches at the top of the curve take blood to the head and each arm.

5 Arteries carry the blood to the lungs, where it picks up a fresh supply of oxygen. This artery goes to the left lung.

1 All the 'used' blood from the body is brought back to the heart through these two veins, called the venae cavae.

Arteries to right lung

Arteries to left lung

Veins from left lung

6 Oxygen-filled blood from the lungs flows back into the left atrium, ready to move down into the left ventricle.

7 The left ventricle pumps the oxygen-filled blood up into the main artery, the aorta. It is then pumped around the body.

WHAT DO KIDNEYS DO?

Kidneys clean the blood, by filtering out waste matter and straining off any water your body doesn't need. This liquid waste is called urine. It leaves your body when you go to the toilet.

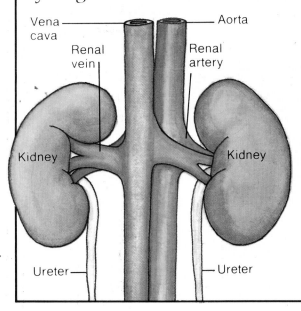

Vena cava, Aorta, Renal vein, Renal artery, Kidney, Kidney, Ureter, Ureter

1 Blood from the heart is pumped through the renal artery to each kidney to be cleaned.

2 Filtered blood flows through the renal vein back to the heart.

3 Urine slowly drips through tubes called ureters to the bladder, where it is stored until you go to the toilet.

You have two kidneys, one on either side of your backbone at about waist level. They look like large reddish-brown beans. Each one is roughly the size of your clenched fist.

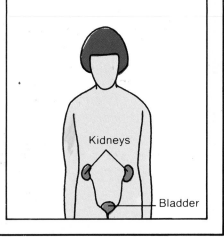

Kidneys, Bladder

WHY DO WE CHEW FOOD?

We chew food to make it easier to swallow and to help our stomachs to digest it. We use our front teeth to bite into food. As our back teeth grind the food up, it mixes with saliva and becomes soft and mushy.

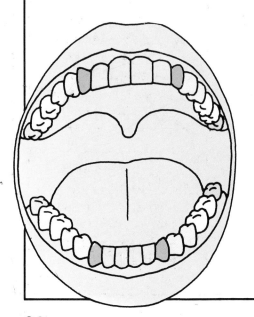

Different teeth do different jobs. The ones at the front of the mouth are sharp and shaped like knives, for cutting. The back ones are wide and bumpy, for grinding.

Incisors – for cutting and grinding

Canines – for cutting and tearing

Premolars ⎤ for crunching
Molars ⎦ and grinding

Wisdom teeth

ACID ATTACK

Sugar left in your mouth after eating turns to acid, which then attacks your teeth. Egg shells are made of similar stuff to teeth. Drop a shell in vinegar (an acid) and leave it for a few days. What happens?

WHAT HAPPENS TO THE FOOD WE EAT?

After you swallow it, food travels through the part of your body called the digestive system. This includes your stomach and your intestines. Substances in the digestive system break the food down into simple chemicals, which are small enough to pass into your blood to feed your body cells.

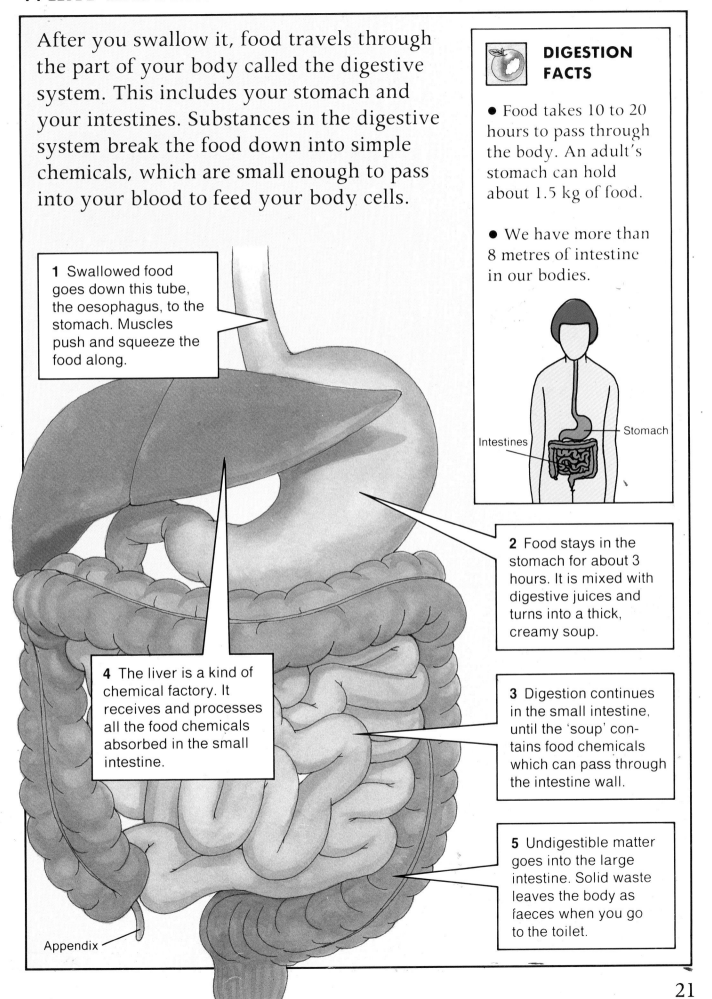

DIGESTION FACTS

● Food takes 10 to 20 hours to pass through the body. An adult's stomach can hold about 1.5 kg of food.

● We have more than 8 metres of intestine in our bodies.

Intestines

Stomach

1 Swallowed food goes down this tube, the oesophagus, to the stomach. Muscles push and squeeze the food along.

4 The liver is a kind of chemical factory. It receives and processes all the food chemicals absorbed in the small intestine.

2 Food stays in the stomach for about 3 hours. It is mixed with digestive juices and turns into a thick, creamy soup.

3 Digestion continues in the small intestine, until the 'soup' contains food chemicals which can pass through the intestine wall.

5 Undigestible matter goes into the large intestine. Solid waste leaves the body as faeces when you go to the toilet.

Appendix

WHAT DOES THE BRAIN DO?

The brain is the body's control centre. It keeps the different parts of the body working smoothly, and it's responsible for thoughts, feelings and memory.

The brain is linked to the rest of the body by nerves. These work rather like telephone wires, sending information to the brain in the form of tiny electric currents. The brain sifts the information and acts on some of it by sending instructions back along the nerves.

 DO YOU KNOW

A large bundle of nerve cells runs from the brain down the back inside the backbone. It's called the spinal cord. Smaller nerves run from the spinal cord to the rest of the body.

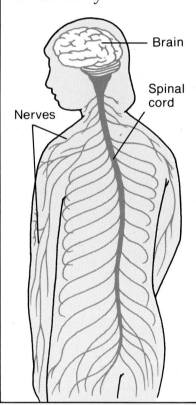

Brain

Spinal cord

Nerves

 KNEE JERKER

We do some things without thinking about them – if we touch something very hot, for example, our hands jerk away. This kind of response is called a reflex action. It's when the body reacts without waiting for a message from the brain. Here's a way of comparing reflex actions with ordinary responses.

1 Sit with your legs crossed and ask a friend to tap gently just below your kneecap. When your friend taps the right spot, your foot will jerk up. This is a reflex action.

2 Now get your friend just to ask you to jerk your foot. This will take longer because the message has to travel farther – from your ears via your brain to your muscles.

 BRAIN FACTS

● An adult's brain weighs about 1.4 kg and has 14 billion nerve cells in it.

● The fastest messages pass along the nerves at speeds of 400 km/h.

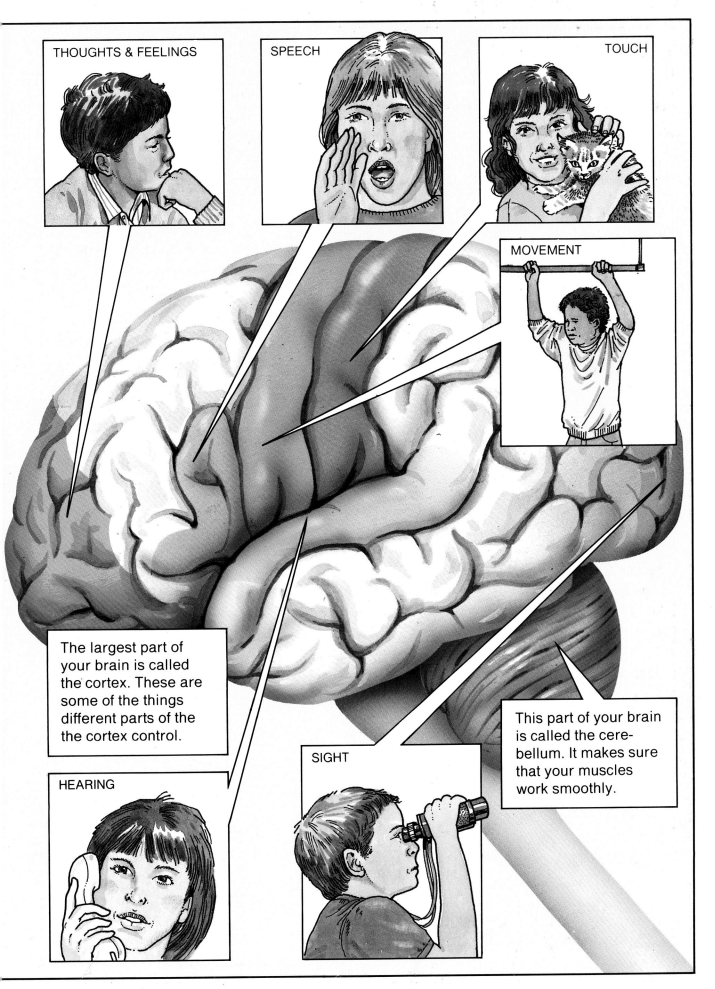

THOUGHTS & FEELINGS

SPEECH

TOUCH

MOVEMENT

The largest part of your brain is called the cortex. These are some of the things different parts of the the cortex control.

This part of your brain is called the cerebellum. It makes sure that your muscles work smoothly.

HEARING

SIGHT

HOW DO EYES WORK?

Eyes work rather like cameras do, only much much faster. Both need light, and both have lenses to make images as clear and sharp as possible. Instead of the film in a camera, however, the back of each eye has a special lining called the retina. This has cells in it which are sensitive to light. Messages from these cells travel along nerves to your brain, which then makes a picture in your mind.

EYE FACTS

● An adult's eyeball is about as big as a pingpong ball. A jelly-like material inside the eyeball keeps its shape, like the air in a balloon.

● There are about 132 million light-sensitive cells in the retina of each eye.

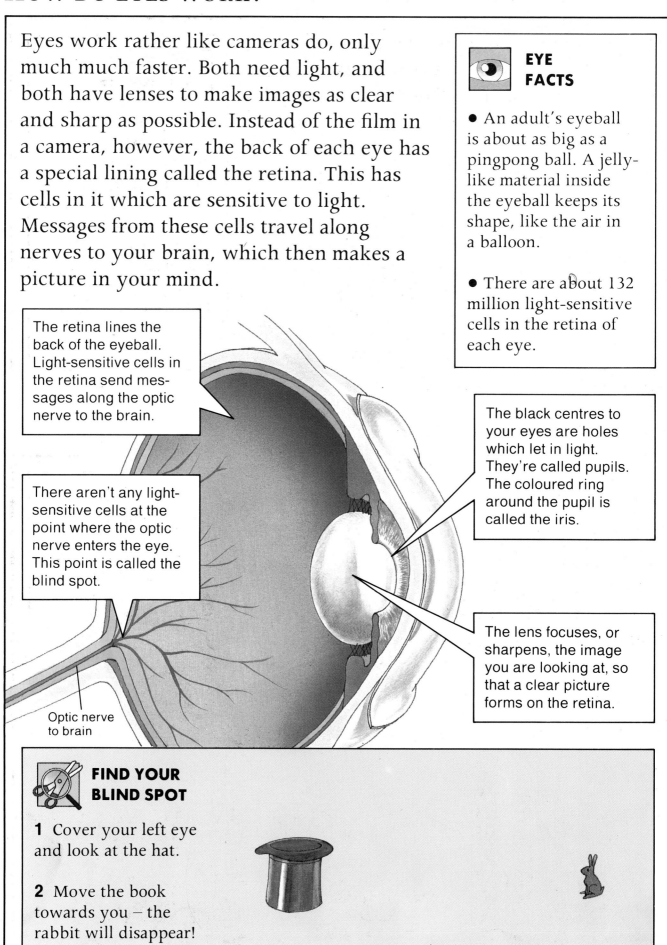

The retina lines the back of the eyeball. Light-sensitive cells in the retina send messages along the optic nerve to the brain.

There aren't any light-sensitive cells at the point where the optic nerve enters the eye. This point is called the blind spot.

The black centres to your eyes are holes which let in light. They're called pupils. The coloured ring around the pupil is called the iris.

The lens focuses, or sharpens, the image you are looking at, so that a clear picture forms on the retina.

Optic nerve to brain

FIND YOUR BLIND SPOT

1 Cover your left eye and look at the hat.

2 Move the book towards you – the rabbit will disappear!

WHAT HAPPENS WHEN WE CRY?

Did you know that your eyes are always making tears? They are washing over the front of each eyeball all the time, keeping it clean and dust-free. When you cry your eyes make extra liquid, which spills out and runs down your cheeks.

Your eyelids and lashes stop bits of dirt getting in your eyes. Tears wash them clean. A tear duct in the corner of each eye drains into your nose.

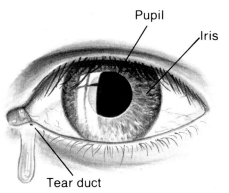

Pupil

Iris

Tear duct

DO YOU KNOW

The iris is the coloured part of the eye. The most common colour is brown, then blue. The iris opens and closes to control the amount of light entering the eyeball. That's why pupils are big in dim light and small in bright light.

WHAT IS COLOUR BLINDNESS?

There are two main sorts of light-sensitive cell in the retina. Rods work in dim light and 'see' in black and white. Cones pick up colour, but only in bright light. People who are colour blind cannot tell the difference between certain colours because some of their cone cells aren't working properly.

DO YOU KNOW

Few women are colour blind, but around 1 in 12 men can't see some colours properly.

The most common form of colour blindness is not being able to tell red from green.

We can only see part of each ear – the outer ear. This collects and funnels sounds into the ear, where they make a tiny eardrum vibrate, or shake. The vibrations are passed on by three tiny bones – the hammer, the anvil and the stirrup – to a coiled tube called the cochlea. This tube is filled with liquid and lined with nerve-endings. The nerves change the vibrations into messages to send to the brain.

VIBRATING EARDRUM

1 Make an 'eardrum' by cutting a large square from a plastic bag. Stretch it over the top of a big tin, using an elastic band to hold it in place.

2 Sprinkle some sugar on the plastic, then hit a metal tray hard near to it. The sugar will bounce around, as the hitting sound makes the skin of your 'eardrum' vibrate.

1 The outer ear collects sounds and funnels them towards the eardrum.

2 The eardrum is a thin sheet of skin which stretches across the end of the outer ear. It vibrates when sound waves hit it.

Messages travel to the brain along the auditory nerve

3 The vibrations are passed on by the hammer, the anvil and the stirrup to the cochlea, which is a snail-shaped tube filled with liquid. The stirrup is fixed to the cochlea, so it passes the vibrations into it. These are then picked up by nerve-endings which send messages to the brain.

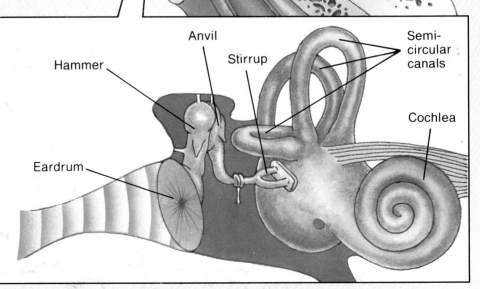

Anvil

Stirrup

Hammer

Semi-circular canals

Cochlea

Eardrum

HOW DO EARS HELP WITH BALANCE?

The three loops on top of the cochlea help you to balance. They are called the semi-circular canals, and like the rest of the cochlea they are filled with liquid. When you move, the liquid inside them moves as well. Nerve-endings then pick up messages and send them to the brain, so that you can tell if you are moving up or down, forwards or backwards, or even bending to one side.

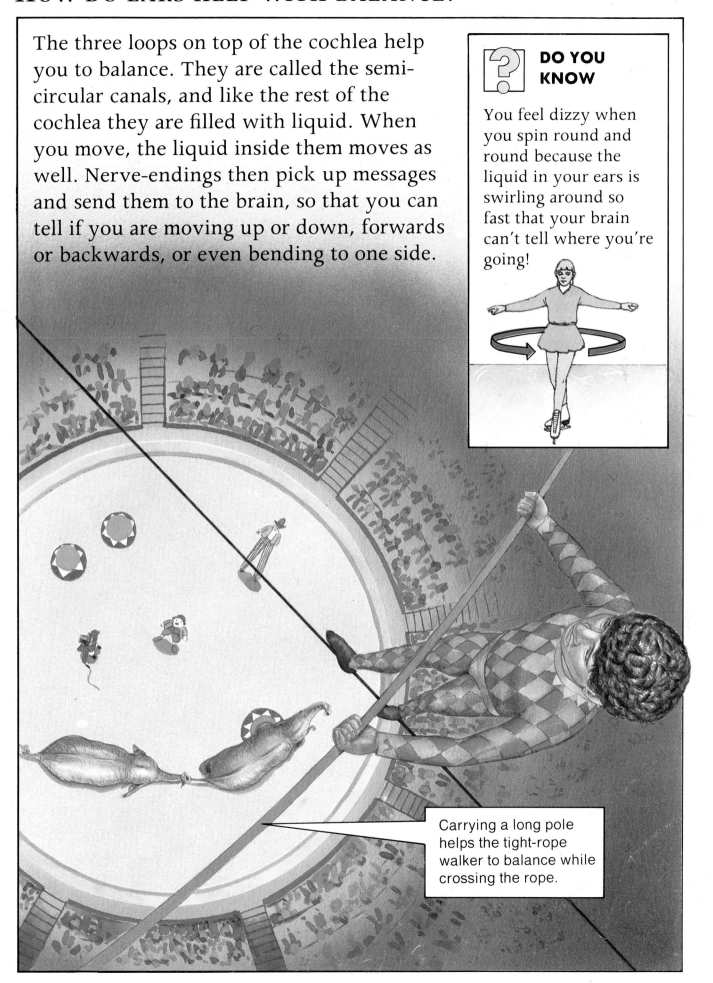

DO YOU KNOW

You feel dizzy when you spin round and round because the liquid in your ears is swirling around so fast that your brain can't tell where you're going!

Carrying a long pole helps the tight-rope walker to balance while crossing the rope.

Taste and smell are senses. We have five senses in all – the others are sight, hearing and touch. It is through these senses that the brain receives information about the world outside. When you smell something, for example, special nerve-endings in your nose collect information about it and send messages to the part of the brain that recognizes smells.

DO YOU KNOW

When you eat or drink something, much of what you think is taste is really smell. That's why food doesn't taste so good when you have a blocked nose.

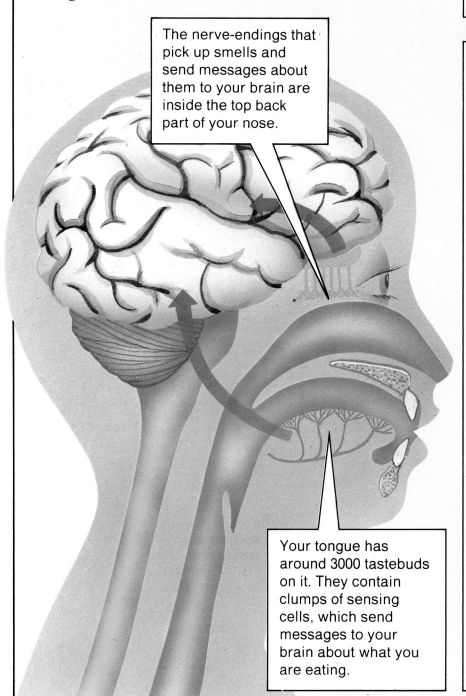

The nerve-endings that pick up smells and send messages about them to your brain are inside the top back part of your nose.

Your tongue has around 3000 tastebuds on it. They contain clumps of sensing cells, which send messages to your brain about what you are eating.

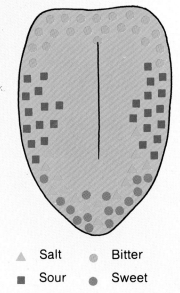

MAKE A TASTE MAP

1 There are four basic tastes – salty, sweet, sour and bitter. Dab a little salt, sugar, lemon juice (sour) and coffee grounds (bitter) on your tongue to taste them.

2 Keep tasting, to make a taste map of your tongue like the one below.

▲ Salt   ● Bitter
■ Sour   ● Sweet

WHAT IS SKIN FOR?

Your skin protects you from the outside world. Much of your body is made of water, and your skin stops you from drying out. It shields you from the Sun's burning rays and keeps harmful things like dirt and germs out as well. Your skin is also where most of your sense of touch is. It is full of nerve-endings, which pick up information about things like heat, cold and pain. They then send messages to your brain about what's happening in the world around you.

 SKIN FACTS

● A piece of skin the size of a 20p coin has over 3 million cells, 1 metre of blood vessels, 80 sweat glands, and at least 35 nerve-endings in it.

● The soles of your feet and the palms of your hands have the thickest skin – about 3 mm thick. It's about 1 mm thick on your eyelids, and 2 mm thick in most other parts of your body.

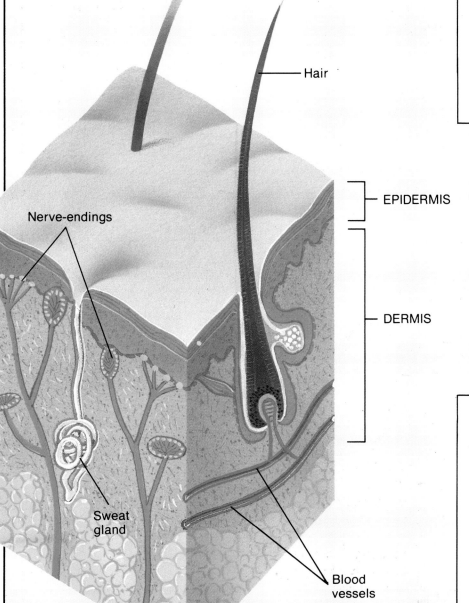

Hair

Nerve-endings

EPIDERMIS

DERMIS

Sweat gland

Blood vessels

Skin has two layers. The tough protective outer layer is called the epidermis. The inner layer is called the dermis. This is where the nerve-endings are. It's also where sweat is made and where hair starts to grow.

 DO YOU KNOW

Even though it feels unpleasant, pain helps us to stay alive. It's like an emergency siren telling us that something is wrong.

WHY DO WE SWEAT?

You've probably noticed that the hotter you get, the more you sweat. This is because sweating helps to cool you down – as it dries on your skin, the sweat takes heat from your body. Sweat is salty water, and it's made in the skin.

WHAT ARE GOOSE PIMPLES?

Goose pimples are the tiny bumps that appear on your skin when you're cold. They show that the hairs on your skin are standing up. The hairs trap a layer of warm air next to your skin – birds fluff their feathers for the same reason.

Goose pimple

TEMPERATURE FACTS

● Your normal temperature is about 37°C. If it falls to 35°C you start to shiver.

● Birds have a higher body temperature than us. Theirs has to stay at around 40°C.

ARE FINGERPRINTS UNIQUE?

Your fingerprints are quite unlike anyone else's. The ridges of skin on your fingertips form a pattern – usually a whorl, a loop or an arch. Everyone's pattern is different. The police can use this to solve crimes. If they find fingerprints at the scene of a crime, they try to match them to prints of people they think might be guilty.

DO YOU KNOW

Palmists are people who believe they can tell what sort of person you are from the lines on your hands. Some claim they can tell the future.

These are the main fingerprint patterns. Try the project below to find out what your finger and hand prints are like.

Arch   Loop   Whorl

COMPARE HAND PRINTS

1 Roll washable paint or ink over the palm and fingers of your hand. If you don't have a roller, use a big paintbrush instead.

2 Press your hand firmly down on a white sheet of paper. Don't move or wiggle it!

3 Compare your prints with a friend's – how different are your fingerprints?

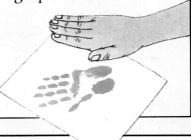

WHAT ARE FRECKLES?

Freckles are brown speckles in the skin. They are made by a substance called melanin, which gives your skin and hair their colour and, as you get sun-tanned, protects you from the Sun's harmful rays. You get freckles when melanin is spread unevenly.

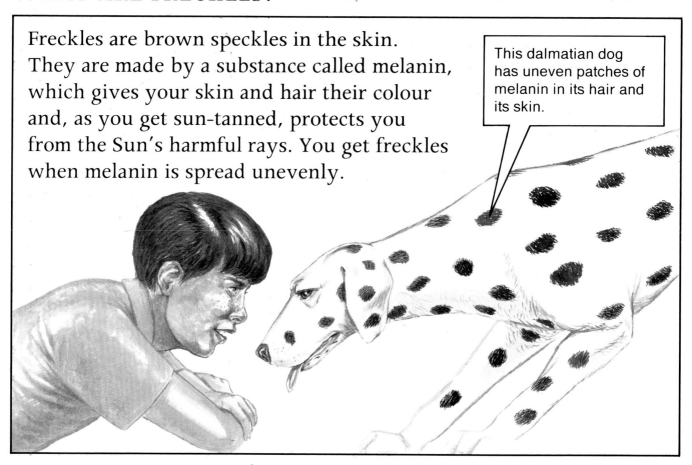

This dalmatian dog has uneven patches of melanin in its hair and its skin.

HOW FAST DO NAILS GROW?

Nails grow at a rate of about 0.1 mm a day – that's 3 or so mm a month. Nails have no nerve-endings in them, so cutting them doesn't hurt. New nail grows from the bottom of the nail under the skin. It is made of a tough material called keratin.

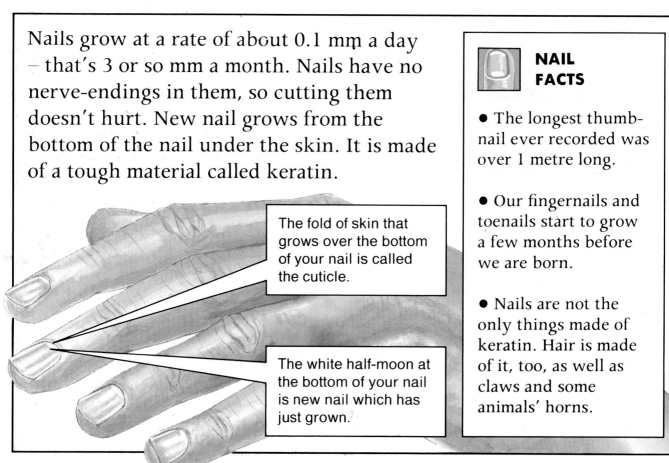

The fold of skin that grows over the bottom of your nail is called the cuticle.

The white half-moon at the bottom of your nail is new nail which has just grown.

NAIL FACTS

● The longest thumb-nail ever recorded was over 1 metre long.

● Our fingernails and toenails start to grow a few months before we are born.

● Nails are not the only things made of keratin. Hair is made of it, too, as well as claws and some animals' horns.

How fast does hair grow?

The hair on your head grows about 12 mm each month. Most people's hair would grow to around 70 cm if they didn't cut it, but some people can grow their hair longer than others. Each hair usually lasts 3 years. Then it falls out and a new one grows.

HAIR FACTS

- About 50 head hairs fall out every day.

- The longest beard ever recorded was over 5 metres long.

What makes hair curl?

Hair grows out of pits in the skin called follicles. And it's the shape of these follicles which makes people's hair straight, wavy or curly – flat-sided follicles produce curly hair, for example. Hair follicles can also be round or oval.

DO YOU KNOW

Most blondes have about 140,000 hairs on their head. Redheads have 90,000.

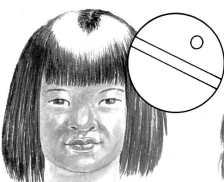

Straight hair grows from a round follicle.

Wavy hair grows from an oval follicle.

Curly hair grows from a flat-sided follicle.

HOW MUCH SLEEP DO WE NEED?

Different people need different amounts of sleep, but most people need less as they grow older. Young babies sleep most of the time, but by the time they're four, children sleep for 10 to 14 hours a night. Most adults need between 6 and 9 hours a night.

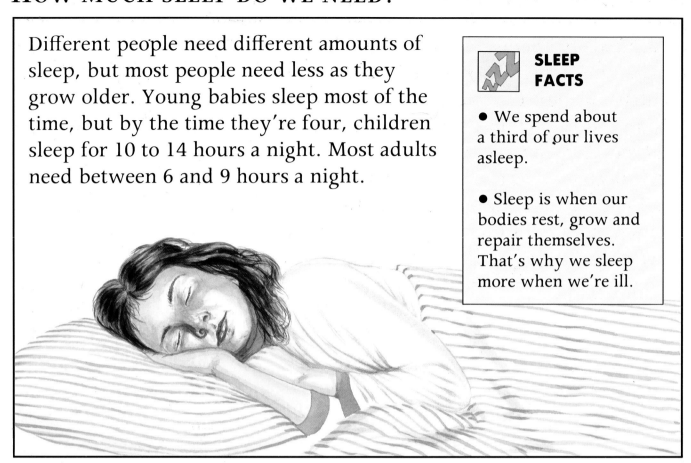

SLEEP FACTS

● We spend about a third of our lives asleep.

● Sleep is when our bodies rest, grow and repair themselves. That's why we sleep more when we're ill.

HOW OFTEN DO WE DREAM?

Some people say they never dream, but in fact everyone has about five dreams a night. You probably only remember a dream if you wake up in the middle of it or just afterwards. Some dreams are very common – ones about falling, for example.

Dreams

Bed time

Time to wake up

DO YOU KNOW

Some people walk or talk in their sleep. This happens when they are nearly awake. They don't usually remember anything about it when they do wake up, though.

All new life begins with just one cell. To make this first cell, a sperm from the father enters an egg from the mother. This is called conception. The new cell grows inside the mother in a body part called the womb. It divides over and over again to make the millions of cells which will form the different parts of the baby's body – from heart, lungs and brain, to skin, hair and fingernails.

1 At conception (right), a sperm from the father enters an egg from the mother.

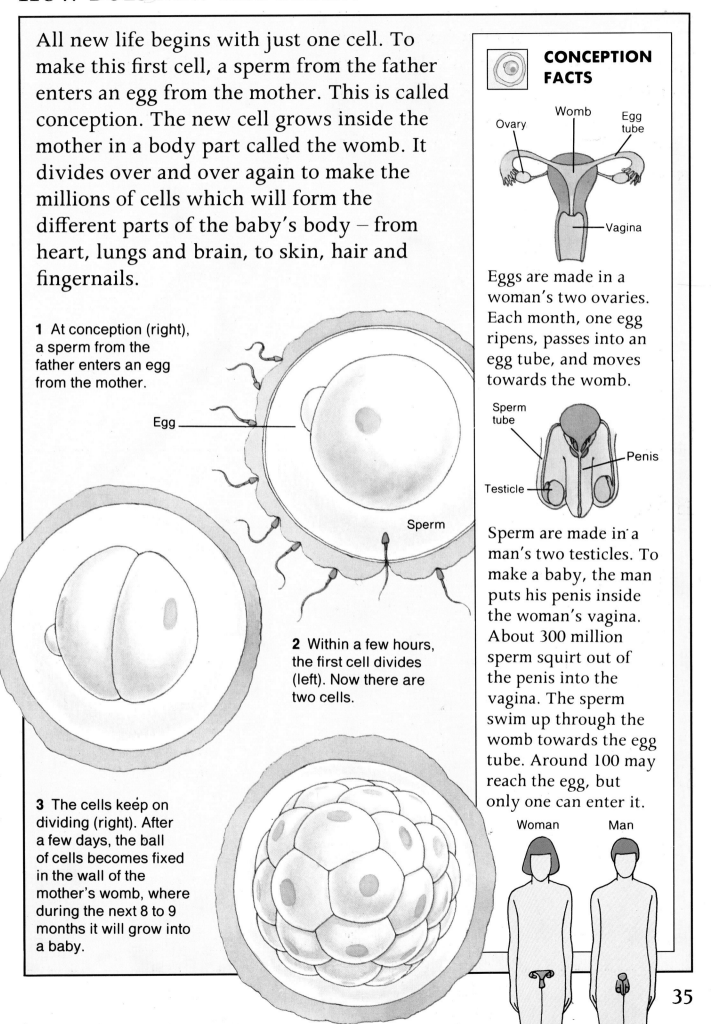

Egg

Sperm

2 Within a few hours, the first cell divides (left). Now there are two cells.

3 The cells keep on dividing (right). After a few days, the ball of cells becomes fixed in the wall of the mother's womb, where during the next 8 to 9 months it will grow into a baby.

CONCEPTION FACTS

Ovary — Womb — Egg tube

Vagina

Eggs are made in a woman's two ovaries. Each month, one egg ripens, passes into an egg tube, and moves towards the womb.

Sperm tube — Penis

Testicle

Sperm are made in a man's two testicles. To make a baby, the man puts his penis inside the woman's vagina. About 300 million sperm squirt out of the penis into the vagina. The sperm swim up through the womb towards the egg tube. Around 100 may reach the egg, but only one can enter it.

Woman   Man

35

WHEN DO WE GROW FASTEST?

We grew fastest before we were born. In the nine months we spent in our mothers' wombs, we grew from a single cell no bigger than a full stop into a baby about 50 cm long and weighing 3 to 4 kg. Babies go on growing quickly. By the time they are one year old, they are about four times as heavy as when they were born. By the time girls are $7\frac{1}{2}$ and boys are 9, they have reached three-quarters of their adult height.

DO YOU KNOW

After about 20 weeks in the womb, the baby can hear sounds, tell light from dark, swallow, and suck its thumb. Some unborn babies even suffer from hiccups!

1 Twelve weeks after conception, the baby's brain, heart and other main parts have already formed. The baby weighs only 18 grams and is about 6.5 cm long.

2 After 22 weeks the baby is tiny (30 cm long), but fully formed. For some time now it has been moving around a lot, and the mother sometimes feels it kicking.

3 After 34 weeks the baby weighs about 2.5 kg and is roughly 46 cm long.

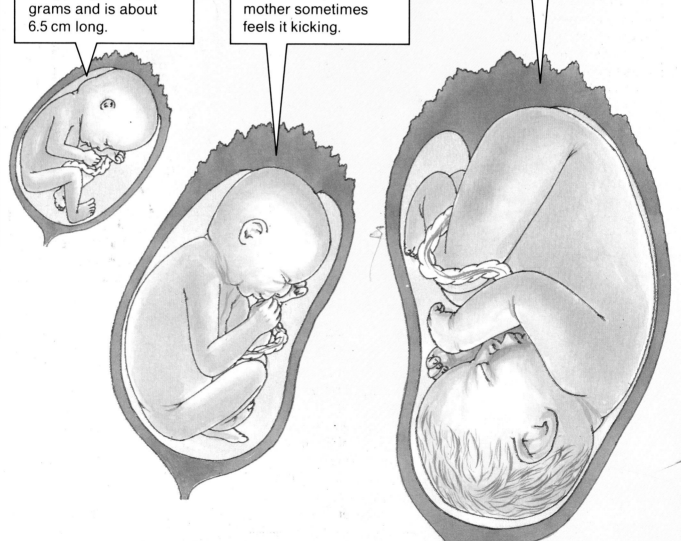
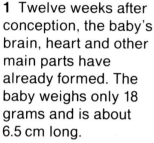

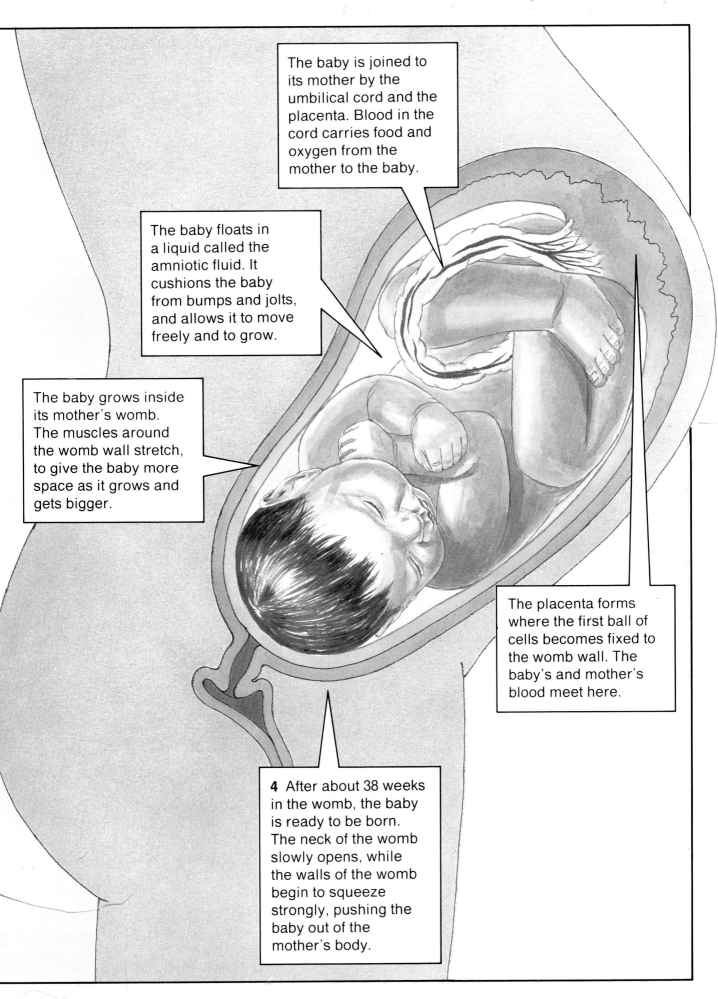

The baby is joined to its mother by the umbilical cord and the placenta. Blood in the cord carries food and oxygen from the mother to the baby.

The baby floats in a liquid called the amniotic fluid. It cushions the baby from bumps and jolts, and allows it to move freely and to grow.

The baby grows inside its mother's womb. The muscles around the womb wall stretch, to give the baby more space as it grows and gets bigger.

The placenta forms where the first ball of cells becomes fixed to the womb wall. The baby's and mother's blood meet here.

4 After about 38 weeks in the womb, the baby is ready to be born. The neck of the womb slowly opens, while the walls of the womb begin to squeeze strongly, pushing the baby out of the mother's body.

WHAT HAPPENS AS WE GROW OLD?

As we grow old our bodies start to wear out and slow down. Our hair turns white and our skin loses its stretchiness. Our muscles become weaker and we can't move so fast. Our bones become harder and break more easily, and our joints become stiffer. Growing old is not all bad news, though. Most people go on leading active and happy lives – and the longer we live, the longer we have to learn about life and ourselves.

DO YOU KNOW

As we get older, our cells renew themselves more slowly, so it takes longer to repair and replace parts of the body. This is the main reason why our bodies start to wear out as we get older.

AGE FACTS

● Many people live to be over 100 years old. The oldest known person lived for nearly 121 years.

● A dog is very old at 15 years, but a human being isn't very old until he or she is about 80.

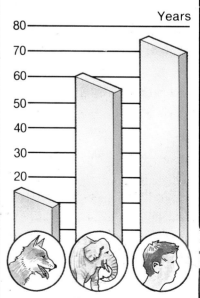

USEFUL WORDS

Artery Any blood vessel which carries blood away from the heart to the rest of the body.

Backbone Also called the spine. The column of 26 bones (called vertebrae) which runs down the back. It encloses and protects the large bundle of nerve cells called the spinal cord.

Blood vessels Tubes that carry the blood which the heart pumps around the body. Blood vessels that carry blood away from the heart are called arteries. Veins are the blood vessels that carry blood to the heart.

Cell This is the body's smallest living unit, and the building block from which everything in the body is made. There are lots of different types of cell — blood cells, skin cells, nerve cells, muscle cells, for example — each type does one particular job. An adult's body has about 50 billion cells in it.

Muscle Muscles make the different parts of the body move. We can control some muscles by thinking about them — the ones in our arms and legs, for example. Others, such as the heart, work on their own.

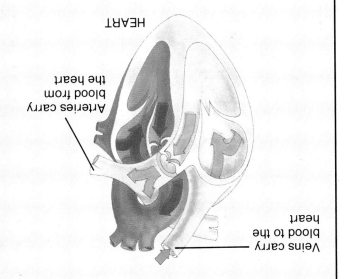

HEART

Arteries carry blood from the heart

Veins carry blood to the heart

Nerve Nerves are special cells which carry messages to and from every part of the body to the brain. The messages travel along the nerves as tiny electric currents.

Organ A body part which does one particular job. The eye is an organ of sight, for example.

Oxygen We take this gas into our bodies when we breathe air into our lungs — air is about 21% oxygen. Our bodies need oxygen to make energy and keep us alive. Without oxygen we would die.

Senses We have five senses — hearing, sight, smell, taste and touch.

Skeleton The framework of bones which supports the body and carries its weight.

Vein Any blood vessel which carries blood towards the heart.

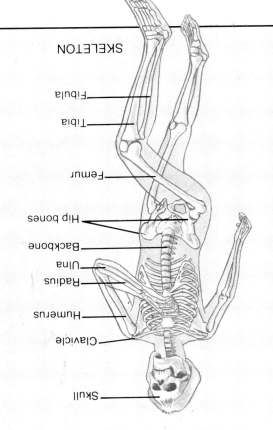

SKELETON

Skull

Clavicle

Humerus

Radius

Ulna

Backbone

Hip bones

Femur

Tibia

Fibula

INDEX